THE WORLD LANGUAGE
DAILY TECH GUIDE

D1622800

THE WORLD LANGUAGE DAILY TECH GUIDE

A Survival Guide

to Using Technology

to Improve Classroom Management

and to Visually Support

the 90% Target Language Goal

for Level One Students

at the Secondary Level

ELLEN SHRAGER

TEACHER VOICE PUBLISHING

P. O. Box 446

VILLANOVA, PA 19085

For information about special discounts for bulk purchases, please contact Teacher Voice Publishing Special Sales at 1-610-355-0553 or teachervoicepublishing@ comcast.net.

MANUFACTURED IN THE UNITED STATES OF AMERICA

LC 2012931437

ISBN 978-0-9793200-3-3 0-9793200-3-8

To my husband,

Ed,

for his steady support and love while I submerged
myself in recreating my teaching voice

and

to my friend

Suzanne,

for being the embodiment of an excellent
colleague and the godmother of my pension

CONTENTS

ACKNOWLEDGMENTS

I would like to thank my building colleagues and my FLTEACH cyberspace colleagues for sharing their experiences with me. Special thanks to:

Sue Alice Shay for encouraging me to write this book.

Mary Holmes and Roya Petersen for assuring me that other teachers are eager to learn how to do this.

Kris Riegel-Martínez and Lisa Hvizda for reading my rough draft and validating my ideas.

Debbie Kelly and Barb Andrews for sitting in a poorly lit lobby at ACTFL and judging my prototypes to be worthy of continuing and for Barb's weekly supportive phone calls.

Suzanne Stone for sharing the daily process and for her creativity, sense of art, and wonder—which make me a better teacher.

My husband, Ed, for being so patient about everything I neglected while I was writing this book. I thank him for making do and picking up the slack.

Renée Nicholls, my editor, for being a genius at making me sound better than I am. I am so lucky to have her support.

My sister, Anne, for encouraging me during our daily talks to try this technical writing. Quite frankly I do not enjoy it like the other kind of writing but she urged me to expand my wings in the hope that teachers and students might benefit from it.

Although there are many fingerprints all over this book, I alone am responsible for any errors.

Dear Colleagues,

What is your excuse for not using 90% target language (TL) in your level one classroom? Here are the ones I used to use when I considered my seventh-grade classes:

- ♥ I use the first few months to build excellent rapport with my students, turning their first exposure to Spanish into a lifelong love for the language.

- ♥ Many students with higher test scores and parental support were steered to learn German, French, and Mandarin. Most students with lower abilities and in need of 504 and IEP accommodations are encouraged to take Spanish; they tend to have a lower tolerance for ambiguity and can act out if they do not know word-for-word what is said in class. I would have more discipline problems if I conducted 90% of the level one class in the target language.

- ♥ I do not know how to do it. (When I attended sessions at conferences looking for answers, I only found **university** professors teaching level one in the target language to students—very little to do with my teaching level one to seventh graders.)

- ♥ Even the "pros" don't do it. (When a "master presenter" was brought in to teach my department how to teach in the target language, she assured my colleagues that in her 35 years of teaching, she

only expected to reach the 90% goal during the
second half of year two of students' instruction.)

While I was thinking it could not be done under my
circumstances, I received a large interactive board in my
classroom. I am a baby boomer, a "tech immigrant" who
threw out a scanner/printer at home because it was just
too hard to learn how to scan. As I write these words, I
confess that I missed the whole Myspace" scene, am not
on Facebook, do not know how to text, and do not know
how to tweet. I can copy and paste using print screen, e-
mail, download a YouTube video, play an audio CD or a
DVD, browse to insert files, and most days—but not all
days—find a computer file that I have saved somewhere.

I tell you this to assure you that if I can learn to use simple
technology in the classroom, you can too! And as you will
see, I soon realized that using technology to help me
teach, which I call *tech-guiding*, was the key to reaching
the 90% target language goal.

At first, I used the large interactive board for PowerPoint
presentations. Then I switched to using its software. Next,
I realized that I could prepare for my lessons in the same
manner I prepare for my teacher-training workshops, with
everything scripted for the full class period, if I had a
presentation remote.

INTRODUCTION

I spent $40 for a presentation remote.

My beloved, but frequently dropped, remote is held together with masking tape.

I also needed to be able to work at home so I bought a large-capacity thumb drive. Before we wring our hands about how much we teachers pay out of our own pockets, I must confess that I had an eighth-grade class at the end of the day that made every five-minute increment feel like an hour. I would gladly have paid $100 a day, not the actual $.75 a day, to keep them focused.

Have you ever taught such a class? You know, a level one class with the following:

- ♥ Students who could not start a language when everyone else did
- ♥ Many repeaters, who do not pay attention because they "know" everything from last time
- ♥ Several students who have IEPs and 504 accommodations and lots of issues with paying attention and behavior

INTRODUCTION

You have? Then you are probably like me; you really enjoy these students one-on-one but together they are a challenge on their good days and a nightmare on their bad days.

Think about that class. Where did things fall apart? If your class was like my class, the answer is almost always "during the transitions."
Since we good teachers know to vary our activities every ten minutes or so, there are more transitions now than ever.

They include:

- ♥ Fumbling for the right track on an audio CD for a listening activity
- ♥ Getting together with partners for paired practice
- ♥ Preparing to present the paired practice
- ♥ Returning to seats after paired practice
- ♥ Taking out the words to the song-of-the-week and playing the song or video
- ♥ Handing out and starting worksheets
- ♥ Opening the vocabulary or some other instructional PowerPoint presentation
- ♥ Writing answers on the board with my back turned
- ♥ Loading up a video

INTRODUCTION

This afternoon, my eighth-grade students in my most challenging class beautifully transitioned to picking up their dry erase markers and page protectors for an audio activity. I complimented them on how well they did that transition, and I told them about this book. They offered to help me compose a list of what could go wrong during a transition. As it turns out, I was unaware of many of their actual transgressions! Their list included:

- ♥ Drawing on people
- ♥ Texting
- ♥ Kicking
- ♥ Playing paper football
- ♥ Fake wrestling
- ♥ Slap-boxing
- ♥ Shooting wasps (hard folded papers/rubber bands)
- ♥ Banging paper (making loud noise with thick paper)
- ♥ Pretending to rip other students' papers
- ♥ Ripping other students' papers
- ♥ Hiding someone's possessions
- ♥ Tickling
- ♥ Pretending to need a tissue
- ♥ Pretending to need to sharpen a pencil
- ♥ Talking
- ♥ Talking with other people's voices
- ♥ Making "old grandpa noises"
- ♥ Eating

INTRODUCTION

- ♥ Pushing/slamming a desk into someone
- ♥ Pretending to steal an item from someone
- ♥ Stealing an item (pencil/paper/book bag/phone)
- ♥ Bumping, touching someone
- ♥ Yelling
- ♥ Burping
- ♥ Pretending to pass gas
- ♥ Passing gas
- ♥ Pretending to throw something at someone
- ♥ Throwing something at someone
- ♥ Shooting spitballs
- ♥ Throwing objects onto the tops of florescent lights
- ♥ Jumping to touch something on the ceiling
- ♥ Jumping to touch the top of the doorways
- ♥ Impeding someone's movement
- ♥ Punching someone in the arm
- ♥ Giving someone "birthday" punches
- ♥ Whistling
- ♥ Tripping one another
- ♥ Clicking one's tongue
- ♥ Getting up
- ♥ Showing one's underwear
- ♥ Saying *boom*
- ♥ Passing notes
- ♥ Playing trash basketball
- ♥ Asking and receiving gum/putting it under desk

Yikes! Who knew? Who would not want to minimize transitions and reduce these behaviors?

When I started to tech-guide my classes, my classroom management improved because a tech-guided classroom almost eliminates transitions; the students transition but I am up and about circulating among them and do not have my attention diverted to the computer or my back turned writing on the board.

You, too, can improve your classroom management—with two caveats.

One, this approach is not based on any theory or research; I am merely sharing with you what I discovered to work for me. If you need some scientific research before trying something new, this is not for you. You will continue to teach with the same activities that you have already found to be successful with your students. The difference will be that you will enhance visual support to your verbal messages.

Two, during the first year, it will take a lot of time. Thereafter, it will not. Each day I need an hour to prepare the Daily Tech Guide for each class. Since I teach seventh- and eighth-grade Spanish, I prep my tech-guided lesson plan for two hours each day. If, like many world language teachers, you are preparing for five different levels each day, then I suggest you do this for the first level or else the class that challenges you the most with discipline and classroom management issues. Just review the students' list of transgressions if you need motivation to spend the hour a day—it motivates me!

Once you commit to creating a tech-guided classroom (TGC) you will realize how easily you can stay in the target language because the slides support the students who do not understand your oral instructions.

I still believe I must teach the first month with a lot of English to help my students who are streaming in from their small elementary schools into our large building. I need to help them feel safe, build rapport, and challenge but not overwhelm them. I will have them using 90% target language (TL) by the end of the first quarter, but not from the first day. My goal is to have them buy into me and my program, acquire a love of the language, and become lifelong learners.

INTRODUCTION

The first month I teach the usual basic greetings and other first-month vocabulary, but I also teach three slides of survival expressions each day. After formally assessing students on these survival expressions at the end of each week, I print them out as individual signs and add them to our "Survival Wall."

Photo of "Survival Wall" from author's collection

If a student forgets how to say something in the target language, we can easily walk over to the wall for the visual prompt. The prompts are numbered and other students will help them by calling out the number of the prompt or pointing it out to the student in need. In my class, number seven is the "no tengo la tarea" slide, which indicates that the student is missing the day's homework. After we posted this, one student would just look at me, shake his head, and say, "lo siento, número siete," which translates to "I am sorry number seven."

INTRODUCTION

The survival slides are depicted and explained on page 31. They include expressions for the following:

- ♥ All class transitions broken into minute details
- ♥ Teacher-to-student(s) interactions
- ♥ Student-to-teacher interactions
- ♥ Student-to-student interactions

Some teachers disagree with this approach because the prevailing theory is to start from day one using exclusively the target language. They do not have the same kind of students that I do. When I hear their stories, I congratulate them for being able to dive in from day one, and I respectfully request that they do not judge those of us with a different clientele. I do not teach elementary school students; nor do I teach college. I do not exclusively teach the elite with high test scores and involved parents. I do not teach only those students who elect to study Spanish; nor do I only teach the college-bound students. But I am blessed because my diverse students enrich my life and enthuse me with hope for our country's future. Someday they may even be able to fund my social security payments through their high earnings.

But I digress.

INTRODUCTION

Returning to the topic of using 90% target language in the level one classroom, what does that mean? Are we talking only about the spoken language? How is it measured? We teachers can control our verbal output. We can train our students with survival phrases and then ignore or redirect their utterances unless they are in the target language. We can drill them with more survival phrases to use with one another, but what teacher can completely control what comes out of the mouths of impulsive adolescents?

Before I learned to tech-guide my classes, I asked teachers how to measure 90% TL in a classroom. Does it count if the teacher uses the language exclusively but only a handful of heritage speakers actually speak in class while the rest are silent for fear of losing points if they use English? Does it count if the teacher and most of the students use the target language exclusively with one another, but students support one another by quietly helping in English the students who do not understand?

If I am speaking in the target language and there are bi-lingual prompts on the screen and around the classroom, is it still the target language? (I will keep the bilingual prompts for at least the first half of the year until I sense the students no longer need them; then I'll remove the English explanation.)

INTRODUCTION

Twice during the first week in December, administrators observed my classroom and congratulated me on conducting a level one class with more than 90% target language. Of course, they were expressing an intuitive feeling more than an exact measurement of utterances.

Let's leave it at that. Start tech-guiding your lessons and you and your administrators will intuitively know when you are reaching your goal for target language usage.

Before you start, you will need a few supplies: a large screen to project what is on your computer, and a presentation remote. Remember, this is completely worth the investment if your school does not provide one. Buy some batteries for it when they are on sale, because once you start using a presentation remote, you will not want to go one day without it.

If you have not used a presentation remote previously, it will transform your classroom management. You will be able to stand in any part of the room—next to any student who needs you close by in order to behave—and change to the next slide. By having everything guided and using the presentation remote, you will have seamless transitions, and you will rarely have your back to the class.

Once you have your screen and presentation remote you will begin to make a <u>Daily</u> Tech Guide for your level one class to improve student behavior and create a classroom with 90% of the target language.

If your school year is 184 days, then you will ultimately create 184 Daily Tech Guides, starting with one day at a time. Mine are entitled "Day 1: Greetings" and "Day 22: Body Parts," etc. Each Daily Tech Guide may contain about 50 slides, because you will be scripting everything in minute detail. By creating 100% visual support, you will ensure that students who do not understand what you are saying in the target language will still know what to do because of the visual support.

If you have access to an interactive board, then you will be able to do this using its software. I currently use ActivInspire software on a Promethean Board. However, I started this journey on PowerPoint and am aware that many teachers only have PowerPoint. PowerPoint is versatile, can be imported into other software applications, and is compatible for tech-guiding your level one class. PowerPoint refers to each page as a "slide" and I will use this term as well. When I use the words "script" or "tech-guide" it means a slideshow in PowerPoint, a notebook in SMART-Board, a flipchart in ActivInspire, etc.

Your Daily Tech Guide will look like no other teacher's Daily Tech Guide as it will reflect your unique teaching style. In these pages I will share with you my version, which reflects my own teaching voice, and understand that your tech-guide will be different.

As you read what I do, be neutral about my classroom activities and focus on the format of the tech-guide, not the classroom activities. One teacher who was struggling with classroom management started to look at the example of the tech-guide, but she stopped on the eighth slide. She threw up her hands in defeat and said, "I'll never give a daily spelling quiz like you—this will not work!" But of course it *can* work. This book is about the general approach, not the specific lessons.

This is **your** process. I hope you will later look back and see today as the first day of your TGC—tech-guided classroom—and that everything before this prepared you for this liberating paradigm shift. Enjoy this new adventure in teaching! If you want to share the journey, please feel free to contact me at mrsshrager@comcast.net.

—Ellen Shrager

ONE

The Daily Tech Guide Example

Here are the 60 slides that comprise one Daily Tech Guide, followed by a detailed explanation. I do not usually number a Daily Tech Guide for my students, but I did so here in order to refer to specific slides in the text. The example slides come from the second day I teach body parts.

ADIÓS LIBROS

ADIÓS PAPELES

ADIÓS FORMAS DE HACER TRAMPA 11

Pásame, Pásenme
Entreguen sus papeles

Pass me, Hand me 12

LA ESPALDA 13

LOS PIES 14

LA GARGANTA 15

EL ESTÓMAGO 16

LA CABEZA

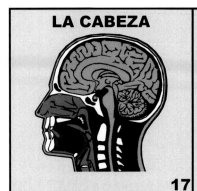

17

EL CORAZÓN

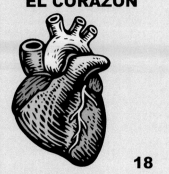

18

EL PECHO

19

[For this slide, the words to the song "La Cabeza" by Barbara MacArthur are written on the screen as the students sing and dance along to it.]

20

BUSQUEN A SUS COMPAÑEROS DE LA SEMANA

FIND YOUR PARTNER OF THE WEEK   **21**

¿Quién es mi compañero/a?
¿Eres mi compañera/compañero?
Decidan quien es A y B

B A

© Can Stock Photo Inc. / lenm   **22**

Doctor/a: ¿Qué te duele? Paciente: Me duele X Doctor/a: Pues,¿ te duele mucho? Paciente: Sí, tiene razón la cabeza el pie la garganta el estómago la espalda el corazón el pecho **23**	**¿HAY PREGUNTAS O PROBLEMAS?** **ARE THERE ANY QUESTIONS OR PROBLEMS? 24**
Doctor/a: ¿Qué te duele? Paciente: Me duele X Doctor/a: Pues,¿ te duele mucho? Paciente: Sí, tiene razón la cabeza el pie la garganta el estómago la espalda el corazón el pecho **25**	**¿HAY PREGUNTAS O PROBLEMAS?** **ARE THERE ANY QUESTIONS OR PROBLEMS? 26**
DECIDAN CUAL ES SU MEJOR PRESENTACIÓN QUIEN ES A QUIEN ES B EL VOCABULARIO  A B C √ √ √ **27**	**¿Podemos ir primero?** © Can Stock Photo Inc. / zurijeta **Can we go first? 28**

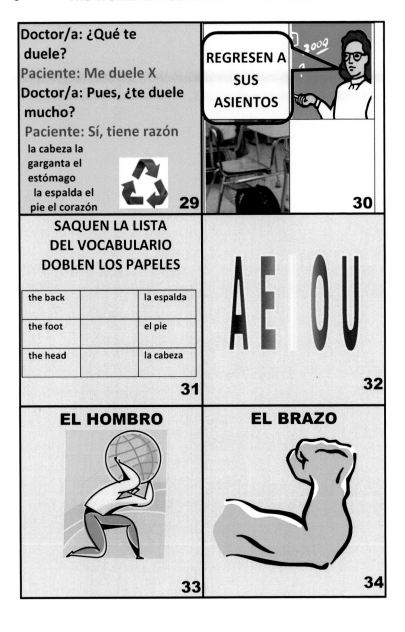

Panel 29:

Doctor/a: ¿Qué te duele?

Paciente: Me duele X

Doctor/a: Pues, ¿te duele mucho?

Paciente: Sí, tiene razón

la cabeza la garganta el estómago la espalda el pie el corazón

29

Panel 30:

REGRESEN A SUS ASIENTOS

2009

30

Panel 31:

SAQUEN LA LISTA DEL VOCABULARIO DOBLEN LOS PAPELES

the back		la espalda
the foot		el pie
the head		la cabeza

31

Panel 32:

A E I O U

32

Panel 33:

EL HOMBRO

33

Panel 34:

EL BRAZO

34

LA RODILLA

35

LA CEJA

36

LA PIERNA

37

EL DEDO

38

You will hear a patient tell the doctor what is hurting. Point to the body part as you hear the patient describe it.

PARTS OF THE BODY

head
shoulder
stomach
hand
thigh (leg)
calf (leg)
heel
foot

neck
chest
elbow
arm
finger
finger nail
knee
toe
toe nail

P 9

39

¿LISTOS?
Pongan los libros
debajo de los pupitres.

40

BUSQUEN A SUS COMPAÑEROS DE LA SEMANA

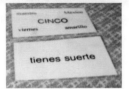

FIND YOUR PARTNER OF THE WEEK   **41**

¿Quién es mi compañero/a?
¿Eres mi compañera/compañero?
Decidan quien es A y B

42

Doctor/a: ¿Qué te duele más X o X?

Paciente: Me duele más X

la cabeza la ceja la garganta el estómago la espalda el pie el corazón el pecho la nariz el ojo la oreja todo el cuerpo la boca el diente el brazo la pierna el dedo la rodilla el hombro

43

¿HAY PREGUNTAS O PROBLEMAS?

ARE THERE ANY QUESTIONS OR PROBLEMS?   **44**

Doctor/a: ¿Qué te duele más X o X?

Paciente: Me duele más X

la cabeza la ceja la garganta el estómago la espalda el pie el corazón el pecho la nariz el ojo la oreja todo el cuerpo la boca el diente el brazo la pierna el dedo la rodilla el hombro

45

DECIDAN
CUAL ES SU MEJOR
PRESENTACIÓN
QUIEN ES A
QUIEN ES B
EL VOCABULARIO

A B C
√ √ √

46

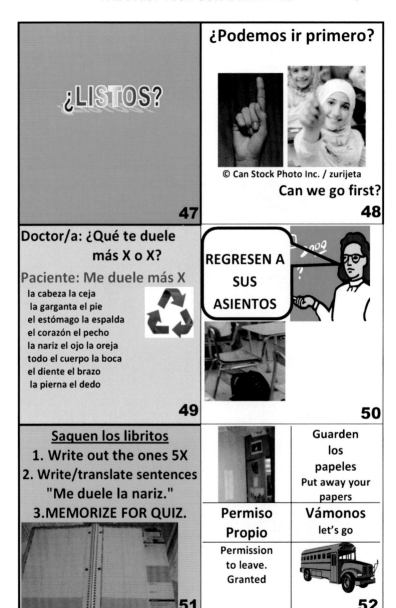

¿LISTOS?

47

¿Podemos ir primero?

© Can Stock Photo Inc. / zurijeta

Can we go first?

48

Doctor/a: ¿Qué te duele más X o X?

Paciente: Me duele más X

la cabeza la ceja
la garganta el pie
el estómago la espalda
el corazón el pecho
la nariz el ojo la oreja
todo el cuerpo la boca
el diente el brazo
la pierna el dedo

49

REGRESEN A SUS ASIENTOS

50

Saquen los libritos
1. Write out the ones 5X
2. Write/translate sentences "Me duele la nariz."
3. MEMORIZE FOR QUIZ.

51

Guarden los papeles
Put away your papers

Permiso Propio

Permission to leave. Granted

Vámonos
let's go

52

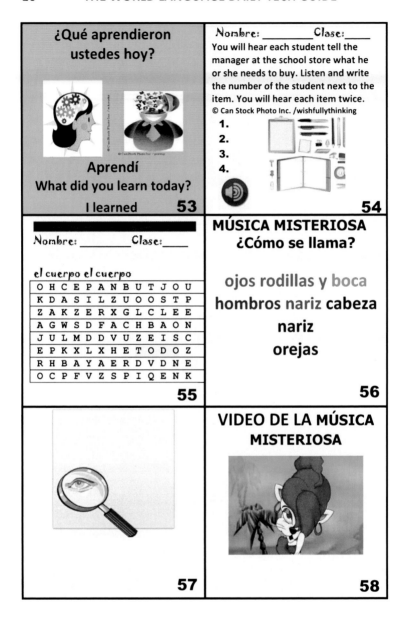

¿Qué aprendieron ustedes hoy?

Aprendí

What did you learn today?

I learned   **53**

Nombre: _____ Clase:_____

You will hear each student tell the manager at the school store what he or she needs to buy. Listen and write the number of the student next to the item. You will hear each item twice.

© Can Stock Photo Inc. /wishfullythinking

1.
2.
3.
4.

54

Nombre: _____ Clase:_____

el cuerpo el cuerpo

O	H	C	E	P	A	N	B	U	T	J	O	U
K	D	A	S	I	L	Z	U	O	O	S	T	P
Z	A	K	Z	E	R	X	G	L	C	L	E	E
A	G	W	S	D	F	A	C	H	B	A	O	N
J	U	L	M	D	D	V	U	Z	E	I	S	C
E	P	K	X	L	X	H	E	T	O	D	O	Z
R	H	B	A	Y	A	E	R	D	V	D	N	E
O	C	P	F	V	Z	S	P	I	Q	E	N	K

55

MÚSICA MISTERIOSA
¿Cómo se llama?

ojos rodillas y boca

hombros nariz cabeza

nariz

orejas

56

57

VIDEO DE LA MÚSICA MISTERIOSA

58

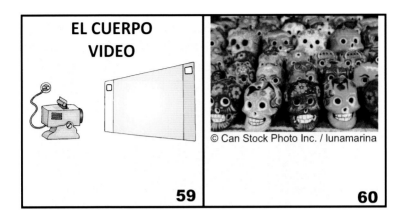

THE FOLLOWING DAY'S VOCABULARY EXTENSION

Now that you have a feel for the flow of my class, I will explain the slides in further detail so that you can adapt them to your own teaching style.

But first, by way of background, I teach a wide variety of students in level one. During the spring, I will make recommendations about which students should go on to the "Honors" classes, which ones should go on to the "Blended" classes, and which ones should start over.

With the wide diversity of students, I have some who run to be the first in the room, sit down, and finish my opening activity before the bell rings, while others still do not have the opening activity started even after the bell has rung and I have walked around checking homework for 30 students. Some of the former students are so compulsive that they ignore my greetings and instructions and then socialize too much when their work is not really done thoroughly. For this reason I do not disclose the "pre-class activity until the bell has rung.

SLIDE 1

I have learned to have a song video playing as they walk in, and slide number one is the alphabet song. If you teach Spanish, the website is:

www.youtube.com/watch?v=TNOo5ZF64hg

SLIDES 2–4 "PRE-CLASS ACTIVITY"

Once the bell rings, I greet the class and reveal slide 2, which has the "bell-ringer" or "pre-class" activity.

Have you heard of a flipped class? As I understand it, if you are teaching a grammatical point (such as indirect object pronouns), you have the students read up on it the prior evening, and then in class you simply practice the concept. This is the reverse approach to teaching the concept in class and then asking the students to practice the concept that night for homework.

I do not follow the "flip" approach per se, but I do give a weekly assignment sheet in class, as shown on page 15, and on the back I have a graphic organizer for the "bell-ringer" activity. I insert on this sheet the information they will need in English. While I tell the students in the target language to take out their homework and start the "bell-ringer" or "pre-class" activity, I am visually supported by the second slide of the Daily Tech Guide. The students receive further support as they silently read the grammatical information in English that they need in the beginning of the class.

Once I invested the time to specifically decide in advance which "bell-ringer" activities we would do for the upcoming week, and to copy the handouts for the students, I found that they took the activities more seriously. I always include pieces of them on the weekly quiz, which frees me from grading them or assigning points to them on the day we do the activity.

This paperwork also eliminates some of the problems that used to occur when students missed a class. In the past, students would complain that they could not answer a question on the quiz because they were absent and missed the pre-class activity. This way, when they return to class, they can ask their classmates about the activity and refer to both the assignment sheet and the handout as reminders.

LA FECHA	PARA EMPEZAR EN CLASE	PRE-CLASS
5 diciembre 2011 LUNES	Explain in English the following 3 grammar terms that we will use this week. 1. "verbo" = verb 2. "sustantivo" = noun 3. "artículo definido" = definite article Most students recognize 1 & 2 but aren't sure of 3. There is only one definite article in English – the word "THE" - used before singular and plural words i.e. the door and the doors. In Spanish there are four ways to say 'the' el, la, los, las. 'el' se convierte en 'los' 'la' se convierte en 'las' ellos quieren decir 'the' ☺ There are two categories of words 'el' words and 'la' words I wish we would just call the two categories "el" words and "la" words but the experts in grammar noticed that "el" is used with chico and profesor and "la" is used with chica and profesor so they declared the two categories to be "masculine – masculino" y "feminine – femenino." FOR ABOUT 90% OF THE WORDS, HOWEVER, IT HAS NOTHING TO DO WITH MASCULINE OR FEMININE EXAMPLE WHEN COMPUTERS FIRST CAME OUT SOME COUNTRIES CALLED IT "EL ORDENADOR" AND SOME COUNTRIES CALL IT "LA COMPUTADORA" Write the article next to the vocabulary word – when you first learn a new noun, always memorize if it is an "el" word or "la" word and the rest of the year will be a lot easier for you. If you are unsure, look at page 22 in text. ____ lápiz ____ pluma ____ bolígrafo ____ hoja de papel ____ libro semanas ____ cuaderno ____ carpeta ____ pupitre ____ estudiante ☻ ____ día	

SLIDE 2

This is the back of my daily assignment sheet, shown on the previous page, where the students keep track of their "bell-ringer" activities.

SLIDE 3

This is the page from the textbook that students can refer to if they cannot remember the vocabulary. I flash it up for them to see so that they can use their textbooks. Then I go back to Slide 2. Some teachers might want to keep it up rather than have their students bring their books to class. We have a classroom set of books, and next year's teachers expect my students to know how to use the textbook, so I encourage them to become familiar with it.

SLIDE 4

Although it is extra work, it is better to create a visual of the answers rather than read them off or ask students to recite the answers. It truly improves comprehension. Use the "window shade" in the Promethean Board and "screen shade" tool in SMART Notebook to incrementally show the answers.

SLIDES 5–8 "FORMATIVE ASSESSMENT"

After a few weeks the students know them well enough that I do not have to put them up, but I do it anyway to remind myself.

SLIDE 5

This slide asks if the activity was easy or hard. I accompany the oral with a thumbs up or thumbs down gesture.

SLIDE 6

This slide probes for any problems or questions.

SLIDE 7

I use this as a backdrop when I ask the students to raise their hands if they are thinking, "I do not understand; I have no idea!" Students love saying, "I have no idea" and will use this phrase unbidden when they are frustrated.

SLIDE 8

This slide quickly follows Slide 7, and I use it in the same fashion. It reads, "I understand. There is no problem!"

SLIDE 9

This slide reminds me to take attendance. It includes:

- ♥ "I am going to take roll"
- ♥ "Here"
- ♥ "Present"
- ♥ "Absent"
- ♥ "Who is missing?"

After a few weeks, the students recognize the vocabulary, but I make sure I include it so that I do take and record attendance online each period, as required by my school.

SLIDES 10–12 "QUIZ AND TEST TRANSITIONS"

The time invested in training students how to clear their desks and prepare their tables is well spent.

SLIDE 10

This slide tells the students to separate themselves for the quiz. One prairie dog asks, "Is there a quiz?" and the other asks, "Is it easy or hard?" When I introduce this slide, I tell the students that even though I give a weekly assignment sheet, post it on the Internet, and mention it in class, invariably someone will ask, "Is there a quiz?" Initially the students do not believe me, but as the year progresses, whenever I flash up this slide, the question is almost always asked.

SLIDE 11

This slide prompts my students to repeat after me.

- ♥ "Goodbye, books!"
- ♥ "Goodbye, papers!"
- ♥ "Goodbye cheat sheets!"

SLIDE 12

When I want to end the quiz, this slide signals, "Pass down the papers."

SLIDES 13–19 "Vocabulary Review"

The first day after I have introduced the vocabulary, I flash it up on the board and the students repeat it after me. The following day I flash it in the form of the extension shown on page 11, where they see the visual and try to say the word in choral unison before the word appears. Here's how to set this up.

In PowerPoint, I would just have one slide and have the words timed to come in from a variety of entrances.

When you import into either ActivInspire or Notebook you will lose your animation and some background graphics.

With ActivInspire, I imported the page and duplicated it, removing the text on the first slide and quickly clicking onto the second slide with the text.

To import PowerPoints using the ActivInspire software with the Promethean Board, use the File button as shown on page 20. I import as objects so that I can edit the text and images, and easily correct any distortions. I do not import as image because then the text and images are fixed, mimicking a "print screen" shot. Then, I locate the file and import.

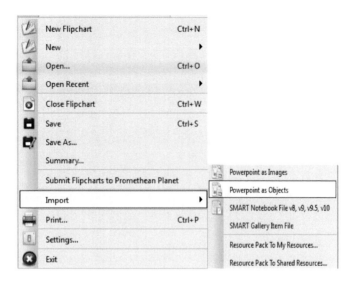

To import a PowerPoint using the Notebook software with the SMARTBoard, you go to File, Import and locate the file. You do not have to choose which kind of formatting.

SLIDE 20 "Song of the Week"
With the vocabulary review over in a minute, the students stand up and divide into two groups for the song of the week. On this slide I include the words to the song so that the students can read and learn. I have imported the audio into the presentation; I click on it and we are singing.

If you are unsure of how to go about importing audio into your software, ask your school help desk to show you how to rip music from your CD. I downloaded RealPlayer to my computer and it rips music from the CD in the mp3 format used by Notebook. I then use the RealPlayer converter to

convert to WMA and WAV for ActivInspire and Power-
Point respectively.

SLIDES 21–30 "Paired Practice"

SLIDE 21
"Look for your partner of the week." As soon as this
flashes up on the screen, my students move to find their
partners.

SLIDE 22

- ♥   "Are you my partner?"
- ♥   "Who is my partner?"
- ♥   "Decide who is A and who is B."
- ♥   "I am A." "Well, I am B."

SLIDE 23
This is the detailed dialogue of the paired practice. I tell
the students that "A" is the doctor and "B" is the patient.
We go over the questions and answers and the
substitution vocabulary is visible at the bottom of the
slide. The recycle arrows remind them to reverse roles and
practice each role at least three times, substituting
vocabulary.

SLIDE 24
Before they start, I ask for questions or problems.

SLIDE 25

I leave this up on the board and they start. On good days, I circulate, but frequently I freeze the board and quickly dispatch with other logistics, like updating attendance and inserting homework grades.

SLIDE 26

When I sense they are done, I ask for problems with this slide, and then give them the 30-second warning slide (Slide 27).

SLIDE 27

This 30-second warning slide reminds them to decide who says what for their best presentation. By doing this, I eliminate the prolonged pauses and I can quickly spot-check a few students. If a pair is not ready, and they waste our time, they lose their participation/preparation points for the day.

- ♥ "Decide on your best presentation."
- ♥ "Decide who is A and who is B."
- ♥ "Choose your best vocabulary."

SLIDE 28

As the end of the 30 seconds near, I move on to this slide, which prompts students to volunteer.

- ♥ "Can we go first?"

SLIDE 29

I leave the dialogue prompt box up for their presentations.

SLIDE 30

- ♥ "Return to your seats."

SLIDE 31

This is a copy of our vocabulary sheet. This indicates that it is time to introduce new.

- ♥ "Take out your vocabulary sheet."
- ♥ "Fold it."

SLIDE 32

These vowels are always up on my board because I point to the vowels as I pronounce the new word. The students see the English word and try to spell it in Spanish. They then flip their paper to check their spelling on the other side. Every three words I pause and give a gesture for the word. I pronounce the words and the students give me the gesture. Then I instruct them to close their eyes and they give me the gesture. If they cannot, I know they need to practice hearing it more and I give them that practice before moving on to the next group of vocabulary words.

(I used to rush them to pronounce but this listening really helps them to acquire hearing the words, in my opinion.)

SLIDES 33–38 "Vocabulary Review"

After we have completed the dictation, we practice pronunciation. I have the students chorally repeat the words after me as they see each visual.

SLIDE 39

Students take out their books and open to page 9 for a listening activity. The audio is inserted into the slide and we quickly complete it.

SLIDE 40

- ♥ "Ready?"
- ♥ "Put your books on your desks."

SLIDES 41– 50 "Paired Practice"

Using the new vocabulary, the students once again meet with their partners and ask and answer a different question. I also inserted Slide 47, which asks if they are ready. I use this so often that they are used to it, but as we near the last few moments of class, seeing this prompt on the board helps them focus.

SLIDE 51

- ♥ "Take out your assignment book."

I make my seventh and eighth graders write down their assignments even though it is online and I give an assignment sheet. This is their chance to ask for clarification. Also, with this method, when delusional parents tell me that their child did not know there was homework, I can assure them that it is part of my Daily Tech Guide and remind them that they are welcome to come to my room and see it on the large board.

SLIDE 52

- ♥ **Put away your papers.**
- ♥ **Let's go.**
- ♥ **Permission to leave.**
- ♥ **Granted.**

Students will pack up anyway so, in order to maintain the illusion of control, I daily give the signal. This eliminates anxious students making rustling noises while I am speaking, a pet peeve of mine. To keep up my Spanish, I watch soap operas on Univisión. I frequently hear this "permission to leave/granted" dialogue and include it in my class. My heritage speakers not from Mexico somewhat mock it, but it makes me feel like the beautiful heiress awaiting the news that my beloved is not really dead and the true identity of my real father!

SLIDE 53

- ♥ **What did you learn today?**
- ♥ **Today I learned . . .**

We all know that a class should have closure, but with the rush of so many students asking for passes or relaying information at the end of class about their upcoming family vacations, I am easily sidetracked and forget about closure. This slide reminds me, and it focuses them while they are standing by their desks ready to leave. Consequently, we have closure daily—not just when an administrator is observing me! This slide helps me to teach "bell-to-bell" and does make for a more reflective class.

SLIDES 55–61 "Backup Activities"

I am blessed that I teach the same lesson several times a day. However, some classes finish quickly. I have several backup activities that I can quickly use before the closure slide. If they are not used, then I might include them the following day as a class activity.

SLIDE 55

My textbook has several listening activities that involve the students looking at a worksheet, listening to the audio CD, and numbering or choosing the item described. I make a class set of these listening sheets and the students insert them into page protectors, which they can write on with dry erase markers. I have a class set of page protectors for each chapter of the book. I buy cheap ones in boxes of 100 and I spend about $3.00 per chapter. It is worth it to me because the students can quickly grab the page protectors with a dozen pages in it and then access the correct page.

In no time we are ready to fill those four to five minutes in class with something interesting.

I buy my page protectors from *www.bulkofficesupply.com* and my purple, low-odor dry erase markers in bulk from *www.dryerase.com*. Many teachers have their students bring in the dry erase markers or else their schools provide them.

To clean the page protectors, I simply cut recycled paper into four squares. Each student tucks one square into the page protector to use as an eraser.

I insert the audio for the listening activity onto the Daily Tech Guide page, so it requires just a click to work.

SLIDE 56
Any worksheet from the textbook series or that you create should also be inserted into the Daily Tech Guide, first as a blank so that you can demonstrate nuances and then with the completed answers. See page 59 to learn how to do this.

SLIDE 56–58 "Introduce Mystery Song"
I am a firm believer that music helps students to develop a fluid sense of saying the words in the target language. My previous students tell me that they miss the songs the most. Yet each time I introduce a new song, students

whine and moan that they do not like it. I ignore their complaints and within a few days, a few are confiding to me that they have downloaded it to their iPods.

SLIDE 56

These words comprise the song "Heads, Shoulders, Knees and Toes, Knees and Toes," which my students have not seen yet. I ask them to help me put the words in the order of a "mystery song" and I drag the words around. This can be done easily on the SMARTBoard and on the Promethean Board. It cannot be done in a PowerPoint slide show, but if you are on the home page of PowerPoint and type the words in as individual text boxes, you can do the same thing, closing out the slide outline on the right.

I spend no more than two minutes on this slide.

SLIDE 57

Next, I have a picture of a head, shoulders, knees, and toes that is covered by a green square. I have made a revealer in the form of a magnifying glass and can drag it across the green square to reveal the pictures. The students identify them and then the order of the song's words become clear.

I spend just a minute on this slide and then start playing the video with the song. (See next slide.)

SLIDE 58

I have embedded in the Daily Tech Guide a version of this musical video, which I downloaded from YouTube and converted to my software using RealPlayer. It plays for three minutes.

These activities together take seven minutes, but if there are only a few minutes left over in the class, I can start it and finish it tomorrow.

SLIDE 59

I purchased a video called "El Cuerpo, Señor" by Etienne and have imbedded in the slide show. It is always ready to go, and the students really like it.

SLIDE 60

The picture of the candy skulls complements some of my textbook's cultural notes about the Day of the Dead. I captured it and put it on a page to keep as a backup discussion activity that can be used any time of the year. I suggest you have at least one of these handy at the end of any Daily Tech Guide. I keep including the same one until I actually use it; then I create another one.

THE PROCESS

To start the next day's Daily Tech Guide, I copy and save today's Daily Tech Guide under the next day's title. For instance, Day 38: Body Parts becomes Day 39: Body Parts. I delete what I will not be using and keep what I will show again. Then I add additional slides as needed.

TWO

Survival Expressions

Photo of "Survival Wall" from author's collection

I teach Survival Expressions for about ten minutes a class period during the first month of school in addition to the usual vocabulary of greetings and basic information.

I teach three slides per day. I give the students a vocabulary list of the slides and a worksheet of the actual survival slides on one side and duplicate slides without the Spanish words on the other side. For homework, they label it in the target language and memorize it. If you create this in PowerPoint, you can use the slide sorter function to print-screen the slides; this process fits more slides per page than allowed by traditional printing.

I give a matching quiz each week on that week's expressions. After formally assessing students on these survival expressions at the end of each week, I add the signs to our survival wall. I use a thick lamination with a peel-off back to stick to the walls.

I realize that the examples are in Spanish, and perhaps you teach another language. Nonetheless, I hope they give you an idea of the visual so that you can make your own and put them in your target language.

You may wonder why I would include some of these expressions. I hand out index cards after the first few weeks and ask the students to tell me what they need to be able to say in the target language. I suggest you do the same.

SAQUEN LOS LIBRITOS Take out the assignment books **3**	**Quién es mi compañero/a?** **¿Eres mi compañera/compañero?** **Decidan quien es A y B** © Can Stock Photo Inc. / lenm **4**

1. "Stand up. Sit down. Please" I use Total Physical Response (TPR) to teach this with the hand commands of raising my palm up for standing and lowering my palm down for sitting.

2. "Ready?" I call this out and the students respond with the same word. We practice this in choral responses.

3. "Take out the assignment books and write down the homework." I use my digital camera to snap a picture of the school assignment books as a visual cue. You may want to include a picture of the cover of the assignment book if it is school-issued.

The first two days I walk around the room tapping on desks that do not have the assignment books out, encouraging everyone to write down the homework. Later, I just call out their names to redirect them. Next year, when creating my Daily Tech Guide, it should be less demanding because so many slides are now prepared. I intend to note who does not have the assignment book and deduct points for not writing down the assignment. I think we do a disservice to our students when we let them rely on the online grading program to view assignments because their parents may be organizing the work; we are not forcing them to be independent participants in their learning.

4. "Who is my partner?" "Are you my partner?" "Decide who is A and who is B. "I am A." "I am B." I assign weekly partners on Monday using random grouping cards in the target language. (These are explained in detail in my book *Teacher Dialogues* on pages 21–24.) We practice finding our partners. I ask the students, "Who is A?" The students respond, "I am A" and "Well, I am B."

5. **"Volunteers?"** I use this to ask for help handing out papers and supplies and to call on students.

6. **"Repeat."** We practice this with choral repetition.

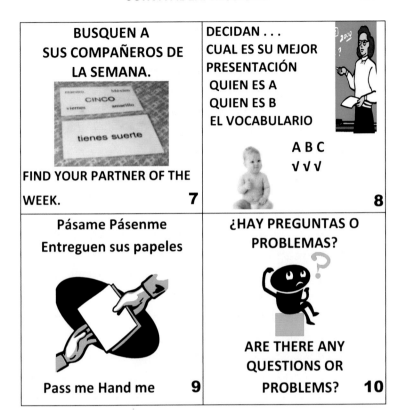

BUSQUEN A SUS COMPAÑEROS DE LA SEMANA. FIND YOUR PARTNER OF THE WEEK. **7**	DECIDAN . . . CUAL ES SU MEJOR PRESENTACIÓN QUIEN ES A QUIEN ES B EL VOCABULARIO A B C √ √ √ **8**
Pásame Pásenme Entreguen sus papeles Pass me Hand me **9**	¿HAY PREGUNTAS O PROBLEMAS? ARE THERE ANY QUESTIONS OR PROBLEMS? **10**

7. "Look for your partners of the week." When the students see this and hear me say it in the target language, they know to move around and find their partners. I let students do this paired practice from any part of the room so that they have a chance to stand, move, lie on the floor, sit on a desk, etc.

8. "Decide your best presentation, who is A and who is B, and the exact vocabulary you will use." I use this as a 30-second warning so that when I spot-check the pairs, class time is not wasted as two students debate who is doing what.

9. "Pass me your paper"; "Hand in your papers." The students practice doing this as a group. Then they practice speaking these words with their neighbor.

10. "Are there questions or problems?" I usually raise my hand as we practice this so that the students with a question or problem know to raise their own hands.

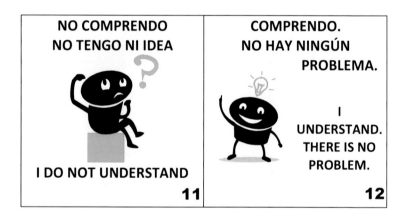

11. "I do not understand. I have no idea." Again, I usually raise my hand to indicate that the students who are struggling can let me know they need help. When I first started teaching, few students would admit that they did not understand me. Today's students are quick to tell me in Spanish that they have no idea; they can do it in a fashion that seems to accuse me of being a terrible teacher rather than implying that their effort is the problem. Bless them for being technically appropriate in the target language while their tone indicates I am in the wrong for speaking too quickly.

12. "I understand. There is no problem."

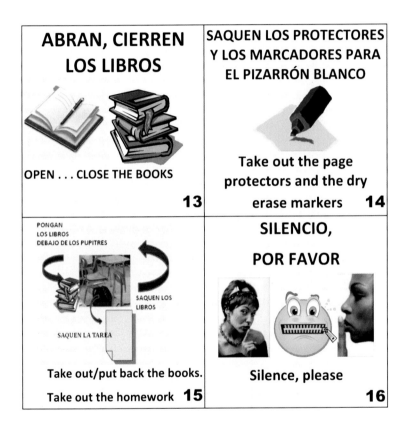

13. "Open the books. Close the books." Students practice using their books. This is then chained with previous commands from slides 1, 3, and 9.

14. **"Take out the page protectors and markers."**

15. **"Take out your homework. Put the books under your desks. Take out your books."** Students practice using their books and homework. This is then chained with previous commands from slides 1, 3, 9, 13, and 14.

At this point we are on the fifth day. I will have the students get together with their partners of the week and practice giving the commands to one another. I flash the slide on the screen, and they practice repeating the commands after me in a choral repetition. Then they practice in pairs. I pick one or two pairs to recite, spot-check them, and move on. Going forward, the students work with their partners.

---

16. **"Silence."** Students enjoy this activity, in which one student asks as many questions as possible, and the other finally says, "Silence, please." At this point, they can ask, "How are you?" and "What is your name?" They try to get in as much as possible before their partner says, "Silence."

¿Cómo se dice "apple" en español?	¿Me puedes prestar? Necesito…¿Tienes…? ¿Quién tiene…?
	un una la una lápiz pluma hoja curita 
Dame la frase…se dice "manzana How do you say…in Spanish? Give me the sentence **17**	Can you lend me? I need…Do you have a…Who has pencil/pen/ the handout/Band-Aid?. **18**

17. "How do you say X in [target language]?" "Give me the sentence." "You say Y." Students like generating as many questions as they can with the vocabulary to date. Some are quite clever at extracting words from phrases to use. Remind them they can only ask a question for a word we have had in class; this ensures that their partner should be able to answer it.

18. "Can you lend me . . . I need . . . Who has . . . Do you have . . . a Band-Aid . . . a pen . . . a pencil . . . the handout?" My vision was that they would learn all of these phrases, but the reality is that they settled on "I need X, please," and they do quite well with that. Students tell their partners what they need and the partner responds by repeating the name of the item and handing it over as the first partner thanks the second partner. As I write this I realize I do not have signs for "thanks" and "you're welcome" because we learn these two expressions the first week and they seem to stick with the students. You should put them on a slide/poster if you have a different experience.

NO TENGO LA TAREA.	LA PANTALLA SE FUE A ALMORZAR
Image of Kwala courtesy of Sarah Thomason/Photo by Samuel D. Epstein	la luz la puerta
I do not have the homework. **19**	no, la otra **20**

19. "I do not have the homework." The students practice this with one partner asking the other, "Homework?" Later on, when they learn Slide 31, they respond back with "Are you serious?"

20. "The screen is frozen. The light, no the other. . . the door" I frequently "freeze" the screen while the students are singing a song with the words or doing the "bell-ringer" activity because I must take attendance each period. When I finish, I sometimes find that when I click on the remote the screen does not move. An acquaintance from Mexico taught me the expression, "The screen is out to lunch." Similarly, I frequently instruct a student to close the door and turn off one light to cut down on glare. Invariably, the wrong light is turned off, so all of the students learn to say, "No, the other!"

¿PUEDO IR AL BAÑO?

© Can Stock Photo Inc.
/ macdeedl / alanpoulson

May I go to the bathroom?

21

¿PUEDO TOMAR AGUA?

© Can Stock Photo Inc. / unkas_photo

May I get a drink of water?

22

ESTUVE AUSENTE AYER

¿Había tarea anoche?

I was absent.
Was there any homework?

© Can Stock Photo Inc. / Enjoylife   **23**

¿CUÁL ES LA FECHA DE HOY?

What's today's date?

24

21. "May I go to the bathroom?" If you teach Spanish, go to *www.senorwooly.com* and check out his bathroom song. My students love it, and it teaches them this phrase like no other. I show them the video, and I also bought the song to add to the mix that we listen to for background during the "bell-ringer" activities.

22. "May I get a drink?" You might want to add the expressions from slide 48 about the pass, but after watching the video from slide 21, the students want to imitate the teacher and tell the student, "no."

23. "Was there homework last night? I was absent yesterday." I intended this to be said by the same person, but when practicing with the partners, the students divided up the phrases, the second answering with a shrug and an explanation. Once the students have learned slide 28, they can add, "I do not know."

24. "What's the date today?" I usually have the date on the first slide of the Daily Tech Guide. Most of the students know the numbers to 20 from watching TV shows and pre-school. Eventually we will spend a week on this but it is a common question when taking a quiz or writing down the homework. I always look at my watch for the date, but my students check their phones. (Except they better be off during the school day!) They usually reply with, "I have no idea."

We spend about ten minutes a day learning the new survival expressions and recycling the old ones. Students strive to mix and match phrases from different slides. At this point I usually put the students into groups of three for variety.

EN VOZ ALTA, NO OÍ. NO PUEDO OIRTE. OTRA VEZ POR FAVOR. Louder, I did not hear you. I cannot hear you. Again, please © Can Stock Photo Inc. / McIninch 25	CONTESTEN LA PREGUNTA ESTOY CONFUNDIDA/ CONFUNDIDO Y TENGO 2 PREGUNTAS ESTOY SÁBADO GIGANTE Answer the question. I am confused and have 2 questions. 26

25. **"Louder, I cannot hear you. I did not hear. Again, please?"** Usually one partner will say something very softly and the other two partners will reply very loudly.

26. **"Answer the question. Are there any questions or problems? I am confused and have two questions."** The first student asks a question. The other two students shrug. The first student then asks them to please answer the question. The second student admits to being confused; the third admits to being confused and having two questions. They can also add, "I do not know" to the shrug.

¿Qué quiere decir "¡Qué padre!" o "¡impresionante!" en inglés?

Quiere decir "cool"
Quiere decir "awesome!"

What does … mean in English?
It means …

27

¿Sabes qué página/ ejercicio/ número?

Lo siento, no sé

© Can Stock Photo Inc. / Colecanstock/jorache

28

SEPÁRENSE PARA LA PRUEBA

¿Hay una prueba hoy?

Can Stock Photo Inc. / jarenwicklund© **29**

¿Es fácil o difícil?

© Can Stock Photo Inc. / jarenwicklund **30**

27. "What does X mean in the target language? It means Y." Sometimes students will want to use the dictionaries to look up words, but I suggest they use what they know; otherwise it can be an invitation to learn naughty words.

28. "Do you know what page/exercise/number we are on? I'm sorry I do not know." Once they learn slide 38 they can also add that they do not listen to the teacher.

29. "Separate out for the quiz. There is a quiz?" I spent extra money to obtain the rights of this picture because I just love the expressions on the prairie dogs. With it on the screen, I am less inclined to roll my eyes when they start asking me, "What is on the quiz?" as I am actually handing them the quiz. As noted, I post online and give them a weekly sheet with all homework, formal assessments, and class activities. Still this question is asked. But with such cute prairie dogs, I do not mind. When we practice this in groups of three, the one asking if there is a quiz today invariably poses like the prairie dog in the picture.

30. "Is it easy or hard?" When practicing with a group of three, one asks the question, the second declares it easy, and the third contradicts the second and declares it hard. My students usually give me thumbs up or down when I ask this to assess an activity or a concept. The students do not necessarily need this slide in the Daily Tech Guide because they quickly recognize the phrase, but I insert it anyway to remind myself to ask formative assessments.

¿De veras?
¡No me digas!
¿En serio?

© Can Stock Photo Inc. / szefei

Really? Are you kidding me?

Are you serious?   **31**

¡MANOS A LA OBRA!

© Can Stock Photo Inc. / grafvision

Get to work!

32

¡Qué chismoso! ¡No seas chismoso! ¡No seas chismosa!	¡Ven aquí! ¡Vete!
© Can Stock Photo Inc/Andres/Flaps	
What a gossip! Do not gossip.	**Come here!** **Go!**
33	© Can Stock Photo Inc. / raywoo **34**

31. "Really? Are you kidding me? Are you serious?" To practice this, one person makes an outrageous sentence, such as, "My name is Lady Gaga." The other two respond with one of these three rejoinders. For my Spanish 1 students, they mainly retrieve "Are you serious?" and do not really use the other two.

32. "Get to work!" I frequently use this to redirect off-task behavior by walking over to the wall and tapping this sign.

33. "What a gossip. Do not gossip." While this slide is never inserted into a Daily Tech Guide, I find myself pointing to the sign frequently because I teach in a junior high. I do not want students talking about other teachers or why somebody is suspended; this sign silences them and we move on.

34. "Come here! Go!" Students make two rows opposite one another, and the row on the left starts striding to the row on the right upon command. When they get too close, students tell them to go away. They reverse roles. They enjoy this.

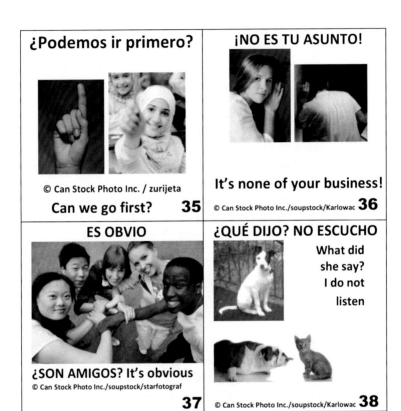

¿Podemos ir primero?	¡NO ES TU ASUNTO!
© Can Stock Photo Inc. / zurijeta **Can we go first?** **35**	**It's none of your business!** © Can Stock Photo Inc./soupstock/Karlowac **36**
ES OBVIO	**¿QUÉ DIJO? NO ESCUCHO**
¿SON AMIGOS? It's obvious © Can Stock Photo Inc./soupstock/starfotograf **37**	**What did she say? I do not listen** © Can Stock Photo Inc./soupstock/Karlowac **38**

35. "Can we go first?" For whatever reason, there are usually pairs who want to perform their interpersonal assessment first while others hang back. When we practice as a group of three, the first person asks the question; the second adds, "Oh, yes"; and the third whines, "Ai, no!"

36. "It is none of your business." Sooner or later a handful of students will emerge as not quite picking up on social cues. They will be hanging around focused on their mission and not paying attention that a private conversation is taking place nearby between two other people, who find them intrusive. To help students practice telling one another this phrase, go to *www.festisite.com/money* and insert your own picture onto a high-denomination currency. (I like the 10,000 peso note from Chile.) Make copies for each set of three. One partner drops the bill; the second exclaims, "10,000 pesos!" in an excited voice; and the third reminds the second, "It is none of your business."

37. "It's obvious." To practice this, two students do something and the third asks, "Are they friends?" The two answer, "It's obvious." My students loved to play act a fistfight and then place their arms around each other as they answer.

38. "What did she say? I do not listen." Oh, how my students enjoy this exercise, in which one pretends to be the teacher talking! Some are wonderful/cruel mimics, depending on my self-esteem that day! The second asks the third what the teacher said, and, with a gleeful look, the third explains, "I do not listen."

¿ PUEDES MOVER?	¡NO ME TOQUES! ¡NO ME MOLESTES!

Can you move?	**Do not touch me** **Do not bother me**
© Can Stock Photo Inc. / magmarcz **39**	© Can Stock Photo Inc. / membio//dabjola **40**

39. "Can you move?" The students practice doing this by blocking one another. In my class, where they are out of their seats a lot and need to see the board, this is a high-frequency phrase.

40. "Do not touch me. Do not bother me." These two are probably their favorite expressions to act out. For the "do not touch" expression, the second one taps the first one on the shoulder as if it were the third person tapping. The first person speaks up and the third person is indignantly innocent. When the second person laughs at the mischief, the first person tells the second it's not his or her business. They are clever about this. For the second expression, I tell them not to touch each other, but to do something annoying to bother someone. They are the masters of annoyance!

41. "I cannot see."

42. "I need help."

41. "I cannot see." When I passed out the index cards and asked students to request needed expressions, many students wanted to know how to say this. For practice, one covers the other person's eyes or else stands directly in front, blocking the student from seeing the board.

42. "I need help." The students pretend to fall and grab one another's arms, declaring they need help. Some students pretend to be adding two plus two and declare they need help.

43. "Do not cheat. OK. Of course not" Usually when they act it out, the person saying "Of course not!" lets a cheat sheet fall or else writes the answers on his or her hand. The rejoinders can be used with other expressions.

44. "May I use the hole puncher? May I use the pencil sharpener? May I speak in English?" Invariably the students assign one to be the teacher, one to be the student who is always given permission, and the third to be the student who is never given permission. They chain these with permission to go to the bathroom and water fountain.

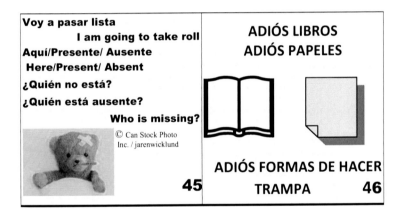

Voy a pasar lista
I am going to take roll
Aquí/Presente/ Ausente
Here/Present/ Absent
¿Quién no está?
¿Quién está ausente?
Who is missing?

© Can Stock Photo
Inc. / jarenwicklund

45

ADIÓS LIBROS
ADIÓS PAPELES

ADIÓS FORMAS DE HACER
TRAMPA **46**

¡Magnífico **Magnificent!**
¡Estupendo! **Stupendous!**
¡Fantástico! **Fantastic!**
¡Qué bien! **Fine!**
¡Buen Trabajo **Good Job!**

© Can Stock Photo Inc./ wacker **47**

Necesito usar la computadora,
¿puedo ir a la biblioteca?
Se me olvidó mi tarea,
¿puedo ir a mi armario? Necesito tomar la prueba,
¿puedo ir a la sala 136?
No me siento bien.
¿Puedo ir a la enfermera?
Sí, dame tu pase, por favor
Con permiso.   Propio.

48

45. "I'm going to take roll. Who is not here? Who is here? Present . . . absent . . . here." One clever group of girls pretended that one was the teacher and the other two were talking. When the teacher asked, "Who is absent?" one giggled and raised her hand. The teacher told her to get back to work while the two friends giggled.

46. "Goodbye, papers. Goodbye, books. Goodbye, cheat sheets." This is the last signal before starting the test or quiz, and all students repeat it with me.

47. "Magnificent, Stupendous, Fantastic Fine, Good Job,." One student says any phrase that we have learned and the other two praise enthusiastically.

48. "I forgot my homework, may I go to my locker? I do not feel well, may I go to the nurse? I need to take a quiz, may I go to room 136? I need to use a computer, may I go to the library? Give me your pass, please. With permission, given." These are obvious back-and-forth phrases, and I added the tradition from Mexico of taking leave and granting permission. Some of the students practice their acting skills with their reasons for leaving the room.

| NO ME AGRADA. 

That's not appropriate.

© Can Stock Photo Inc. / wacker**49** | VAMOS A REPASAR. PROFESORA, REPITA MÁS DESPACIO, POR FAVOR.

We are going to review.
Profesora, please repeat it
more slowly
© Can Stock Photo Inc. / dusan964/   **50** |

49. "That's not appropriate." Two students act out bad behavior. The third takes the role of the teacher and tells them it was not appropriate. They can be gross!

50. "We are going to review." "Profesora, please repeat it more slowly." The student who can speak the most quickly says, "We are going to review." The second student requests the slow down, and the third pleads with the word "please" and "I have no idea." Initially I did not think I would use this slide in the Daily Tech Guide, just on the reference wall, but I do use it to indicate reviewing for a quiz or test.

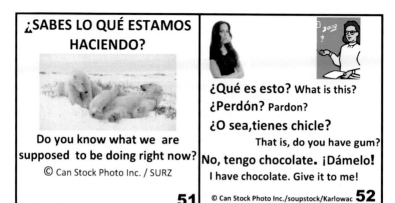

¿SABES LO QUÉ ESTAMOS HACIENDO?

Do you know what we are supposed to be doing right now?
© Can Stock Photo Inc. / SURZ

51

¿Qué es esto? What is this?
¿Perdón? Pardon?
¿O sea, tienes chicle? That is, do you have gum?
No, tengo chocolate. ¡Dámelo!
I have chocolate. Give it to me!
© Can Stock Photo Inc./soupstock/Karlowac **52**

51. "Do you know what we are supposed to be doing right now?" This expression was requested by the students on the index cards. The first student asks the question and the second student answers from slide 28, "I am sorry, I do not know." The third either explains what the activity is or replies that he or she has no idea.

52. "What is this?" "Pardon?" "Are you chewing gum?" "No, I have chocolate." "Give it to me." Eating in class is an issue at the middle school level. Towards the end of the year, I also use these phrases when confiscating cell phones. They always insist they must chew gum for this performance piece.

53. "Return to your seats."

54. "Form a line, please." The students pretend to mill around and then race to see how quickly they can form a line compared to my other classes. We form lines for different activities and fire drills; I need them to be able to do it quickly.

55. "Put away your papers. With permission, given. Let's go." This slide is usually shown quickly before slide 58 as part of our closure routine.

56. "Indicate. Listen. Draw. Write. Touch. Look. Listen." I paid extra for permission to use this artwork because I have it around my room with the different command forms—singular and plural—as a visual reminder to me to not "dumb down" my language but to use the natural flow. Since I only teach level one, I fear that my language skills can get rusty, so I like the reminders.

57. "Are you ready? Everyone? What did you talking about? It's your turn. It's my turn. I go first." I do not play many games in the classroom but on the rare occasion, I put up the cues for the game as we play it.

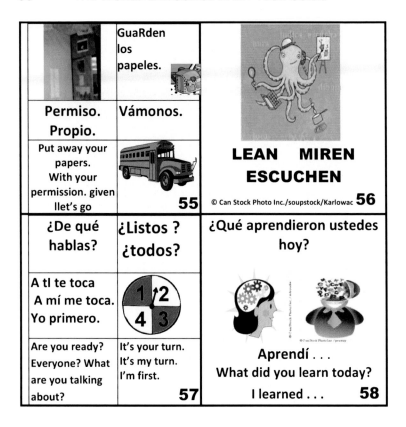

	GuaRden los papeles.	
Permiso. Propio.	**Vámonos.**	**LEAN MIREN ESCUCHEN**
Put away your papers. With your permission. given llet's go	(bus image) **55**	© Can Stock Photo Inc./soupstock/Karlowac **56**
¿De qué hablas?	**¿Listos ? ¿todos?**	**¿Qué aprendieron ustedes hoy?**
A tl te toca A mí me toca. Yo primero.	(spinner 1 2 4 3)	
Are you ready? Everyone? What are you talking about?	It's your turn. It's my turn. I'm first. **57**	**Aprendí . . .** **What did you learn today?** I learned . . . **58**

58. "What did you learn today? I learned . . ." By using this slide towards the end of each Daily Tech Guide, I ensure that there is a closure to the class. This is the students' signal that we are a minute away from the bell.

As you can see, I started with the "top 50" and kept on adding; you will, too!

THREE

Textbook Ancillaries and Worksheets

If you use a textbook, you will need to insert it and its ancillaries into your Daily Tech Guide software. I do not know which textbook you are using, but my textbook has a CD with all of the components listed by chapter in PDF format, videos on DVD and audio on CD.

For me, there are more components than time available to use them. I copied and pasted only the ones I use into my software. I had not really worked with Adobe PDFs before and was frustrated that I could not right-click to copy. Once I learned to go to Edit, Copy File to Clipboard it became a lot faster!

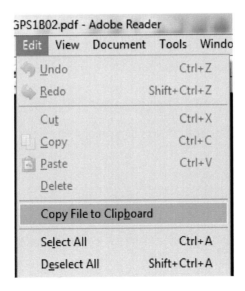

You may decide that when you plan your lesson each week or day you will go to the CD, find the PDF, and insert it into the Daily Tech Guide you are creating. Personally, I just do not have the time during the school day to do that.

Instead, I did this over the summer. It took about 30 hours to do nine chapters of a Level 1 book. (Each chapter in my series has an A and B section, so it was actually 18 chapters: about 45 minutes per chapter.) Some schools have tech people and interns who can do it for you.

If you are lucky, maybe you can divide the work with a colleague in your building or one you have met at a conference who uses the same software and the same textbook. Perhaps the weekend before you start a new chapter you will upload everything as part of your lesson planning. You can always contact me and we can create groups to help one another.

For me, I like not having to deal with the CD. Now I just open my Daily Tech Guide and open the folder on my thumb drive with all of the components already pasted into the ActivInspire software. I can use the browser to see all of the available slides and copy and paste the page into the Daily Tech Guide. In contrast, when I use the CD, I need to have the book and workbooks with me to know which PDF to open because their labels do not match the content of the activity, rather the location.

For example, PW 3-5 is the fifth page in Chapter 3 of the Practice Workbook, but I do not recognize the contents from that title.

You decide what works best for you. In my folder for each chapter, I have ActivInspire flip charts for the following:

- ♥ Audio clips
- ♥ Grammar videos
- ♥ Guided Practice Pages (blanks and with answers)
- ♥ Practice Workbook (blanks and with answers
- ♥ Textbook PPT of pages
- ♥ Textbook answers
- ♥ Writing, Audio, and Video Workbook (blanks and with answers)
- ♥ Videos with story

The practice workbook has all of the answers in a chart. I believe the students make better corrections and learn more when the answer page looks like their worksheet. So I take the time in the summer to duplicate the page and either write in or type on the answers.

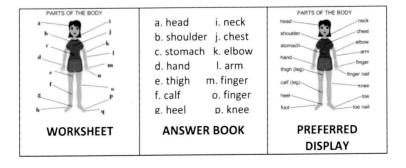

If you are like me, you will be surprised by the amount of extra time you will have in class compared to previous years due to all of the time you have gained by revealing the answers to activities on slides. This approach is much faster than writing them out or you and the students reading them and having some ask you to repeat. You can still go around the room and have students give their answers; just support their answers with the visual. Use the "window shade" in ActivInspire and the "screen shade" tool in SMART Notebook to show the answers incrementally. If you want to do the same in PowerPoint, insert a rectangle shape, color it black, and size it for each slide.

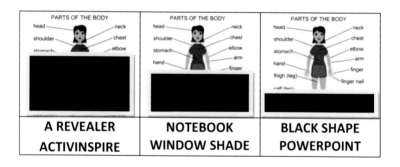

A REVEALER ACTIVINSPIRE	NOTEBOOK WINDOW SHADE	BLACK SHAPE POWERPOINT

WINDOW SHADE SCREEN SHADE BLACK SHAPE

Insert all handouts you create or find on the Internet into the Daily Tech Guide as you use them. Insert all answers to quizzes and tests, actually anything you review, to provide visual support.

When I give a test, if there is a hard-to-interpret clipart picture, I project it on the screen with the correction. For example, one picture is supposed to depict taking a train:

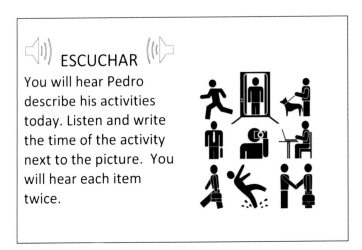

To clarify this, I wrote it in English:

Similarly, if there is a mistake, I write a note on the board to let students know:

Nombre:_____   **Examen:**_____
Shragervilla_____   **Fecha:**_____

#36 is missing 2 answers
D. la boca   E. la pierna

When I tell students in the target language to turn to page 9, the page number added in a large font on top of a snapshot of the actual page cues the students who do not know their numbers and eliminates their grunts and groans of frustration.

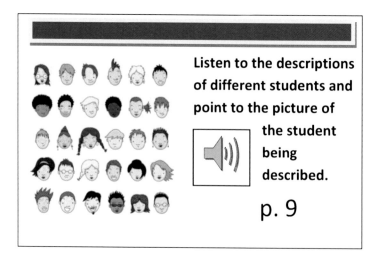

Listen to the descriptions of different students and point to the picture of the student being described.

p. 9

Last year I did not know how to scan my favorite worksheets, because previously I had simply photocopied them onto plastic transparencies for the overhead projector. I discovered that our school library has a very easy scanner that is always hooked up, and it has clear instructions taped to the wall. I was surprised how simple it was; it was not the big task that I had always imagined. I also ask the student library aides to scan for me and put the images on my thumb drive.

FOUR

When I Cannot Turn My Back to Them

"My name is Ellen, and I have taught for over twenty-five years, yet I have one class that I cannot turn my back on without incident."

This is unfortunate because grammar teaching is more colorful and dramatic when I use the interactive board's electronic pen to create sentences, and my back must be turned to do so.

For example, as a "bell-ringer" activity, the students can make four sentences from this slide, such as "She is organized," or "They are organized."

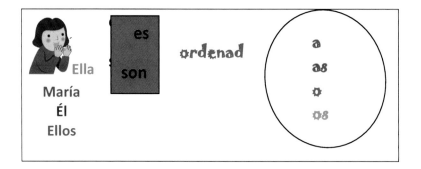

To help them check their answers, I can use the electronic pen to drag the verb choice of "es" or "son" and place it next to the subject. Then I can drag the stem of the adjective down and students can help decide which ending from the yellow oval to use. It is easy because the dragged items are in a 'lock and drag' mode, meaning every time I touch the pen to the word, it creates a duplicate copy while the original remains intact. The duplicate copy can be swirled around the board until it settles in its proper location.

In most classes, even though my back is turned towards them, students are highly engaged in this activity.

However, with this one class, I am reluctant to turn my back because of one particular student, and I am equally reluctant to have a student go to the board because he or she risks taunting for volunteering. I want the students to benefit from this kind of activity but how do I do this without turning my back?

The solution is to prepare extra slides that mimic moving the parts with the electronic pen, without using the electronic pen. It reminds me of one of those flipbooks with still pictures that appear to be moving as the pages are quickly flipped.

It requires an extra fifteen minutes of making four extra slides per sentence, compared to using the electronic pen, but is worth the effort to engage the students. I quickly click the remote presentation device as I pronounce the words with the students usually supplying the words with me. Below is an example.

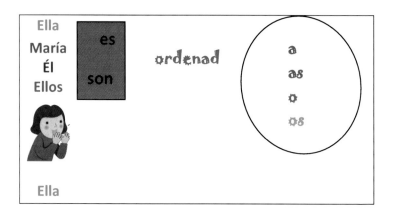

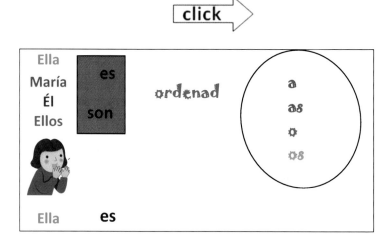

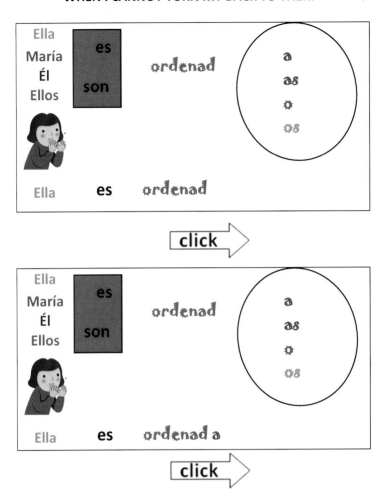

This works so well with my behaviorally challenged class, that I use this system for other topics with all of my classes.

For example, my students complete a worksheet on translating sentences from Spanish to English, focusing on conjugating the verbs correctly. I could put all of the answers up on the board, like this:

> **He reads on Saturdays. Él lee los sábados.**
> **She works a lot. Ella trabaja mucho.**
> **They run well. Ellos corren mucho.**
> **They swim sometimes. Ellos nadan a veces.**
> **She writes a lot. Ella escribe mucho.**

But, a series of slides is more effective with my students.

He reads on Saturdays.	click	Él lee los sábados.	click
She works a lot.	click	Ella trabaja mucho.	click
They run well.	click	Ellos corren bien.	click
They swim some times.	click	Ellos nadan a veces.	click
She writes a lot.	click	Ella escribe mucho.	click

Of course, the students must be accountable for answering every question for this system to work.

They can complete a worksheet and check their answers. However, there are other formative assessments they can use to add variety. For example, students can:

- ♥ Hold up coded index cards
- ♥ Hold up laminated flash cards
- ♥ Call out the correct answers
- ♥ Write on page protectors with markers
- ♥ Stand up or sit down if the answer is A or B

Train your students not to give the answer until you give the signal "everyone," so that the slower ones have time to process.

Remind students that some of us confuse fast processing with being smart, but it has nothing to do with retaining information. Tell them, "Be grateful if you can process quickly, but be respectful of others who need more time to process. Do not destroy their process by blurting out the answers."

As explained previously on page 27, I have a class set of page protectors with a piece of paper inserted in each one. The students use tissues or recycled squares of papers to wipe off the words they write on the page protectors with low-odor dry erase markers. If your school does not supply them, the best value ones are purple and come in bulk from the folks at www.dryerase.com.

I show the first slide, click on the second slide with the 'todos' prompt. (This is the Spanish word for 'everyone.')

This prompts the students to hold up their individual answers at this point. Then, after everyone has lifted their answers and I have spot-checked their work, I click on the third slide, revealing the correct answer. The students moan if wrong, whoop if correct. For some reason they just cannot resist being engaged.

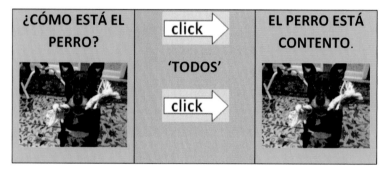

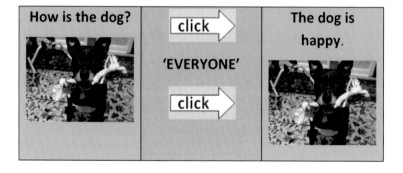

I use this sequence several times a week, understanding that eight questions is the optimal number; more than

that and they are off-task. Below are more examples in
English to help you to create your own

Today is Monday and tomorrow?	click 'EVERYONE' click	**Tomorrow is Tuesday.**
Tomorrow is Friday and today?	click 'EVERYONE' click	**Today is Thursday.**
Today is Monday and yesterday was?	click 'EVERYONE' click	**Yesterday was Sunday.**

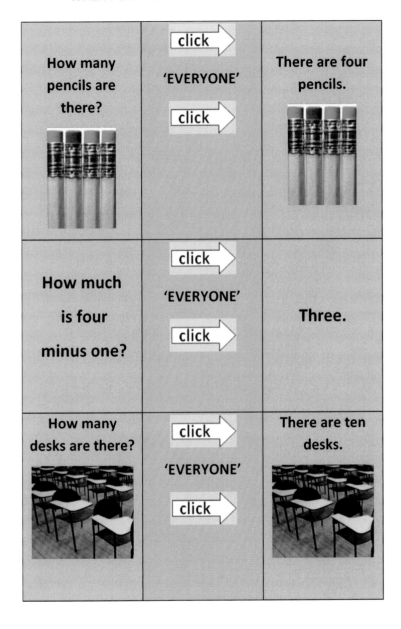

Today is Monday and tomorrow?	click 'EVERYONE' click	Tomorrow is Tuesday.
Tomorrow is Friday and today?	click 'EVERYONE' click	Today is Thursday.
Today is Monday and yesterday was?	click 'EVERYONE' click	Yesterday was Sunday.

In conclusion, my Daily Tech Guide has helped me so much with this challenging class that the only thing more difficult than finding an hour a day to create a Daily Tech Guide is to spend a class period without it. Now I can stand anywhere and teach, using my remote presentation device.

If there is interest sharing these lessons on the wiki, please contact me at mrsshrager@comcast.net

IN CONCLUSION

Using technology for the sake of technology and not for improving student learning is a meaningless waste of time.

Hence, I am not a believer in having two students up at the board while the rest of the class is off task. Some folks are convinced that this approach is what makes a board an "interactive board." I know that everyone writing on and holding up a page protector or a white board is much more interactive.

My department received our interactive boards several years after the other teachers received their interactive boards. I badgered my colleagues to find out how to use it and what they were doing—besides playing review games and using their PowerPoint slides. I was disappointed that few had much to offer. I even asked my students what they saw and it was mostly review games and a glorious two minutes selecting pen colors at the board for their turn to write on it.

My colleague, Suzanne, and I sacrificed our prep periods every day to meet with the tech mentor assigned to our building. He kept coming up with new review games, even though we kept asking, "How do you *teach*, not *review* with this?" A chance conversation with my colleague from the high school, Katie, revealed that her goal was to have three slides per lesson. I was so past that number that I was ashamed to admit that apparently I have nothing better to do than to make slides to guide my class.

But, that conversation spurred me on and the Daily Tech Guide was born. I hope it also allows you to support using the target language in your class—and to manage that class that you don't ever want to turn your back on.

Please contact me at *mrsshrager@comcast.net* if you want to share lesson plans with me or with others, or if you have any questions.

Oh, and thanks for being the kind of teacher who takes time out of your personal life to improve your teaching craft. Our profession really needs you to keep our classes viable and language learning alive and vibrant during this period of budget reductions. Thanks for fighting that good fight.

—Ellen Shrager

APPENDIX A

Checklist for Software Help Desk

I do not know which version of the software you may be using. I would call the Software Help Desk and ask them:

1. What is the best format for videos?

2. Are they embedded or are they just linked, and if removed from the machine with the video file, will they still play?

3. What is the best format for audio?

4. Is the audio linked or embedded?

5. Does it matter if I drag the files or is there an advantage to using the insert and browse file features?

6. How do I crop using this software? (I kept using print-screen because I thought ActivInspire's camera was too difficult. Once someone showed me how to use it, everything became much easier.)

APPENDIX B

Checklist for School Help Desk

I do not know your school's technology department. Once I presented in a school in Oklahoma on a Saturday and was assured that the "tech guy" would be available to resolve any problems. He was fantastic, but he eventually admitted he was the principal. I was embarrassed to share that we have four full-time professionals at our help desk.

1. Can I download the software at home so that I can prepare my Daily Tech Guides at home?

2. How do I rip the audio from a CD or transfer it from ITunes to my software?

3. How do I download a video from the internet and insert it into my software to play when I click on that page?

4. Can you convert my DVDs to a format compatible with my Daily Tech Guides?

5. Is there someone who can help me to insert the PDFs from the textbooks onto the software?

6. How much space am I allowed for saving these bulky files? Can my personal drive be enlarged or should I use the Teacher's drive?

7. Do we get a discount on thumb drives or little hard drives? What do you suggest I do for file storage?

A SCHOOL GUIDE
TO IDENTIFYING AND NEUTRALIZING
"ENTERTAINMENT BULLYING"

FOUR
MINUTES
A DAY

A PARENT AND TEACHER
SURVIVAL GUIDE FOR VICTIMS OF
"ENTERTAINMENT BULLYING"
IN SCHOOL HALLWAYS

by E. C. Bernard

FOUR MINUTES A DAY

BY E. C. BERNARD

A BLUEPRINT FOR PROTECTING THE VICTIMS OF BULLYING WITH ADVICE FOR PARENTS, TEACHERS, AND SCHOOL ADMINISTRATORS

"My son has been the target of constant teasing starting from the first day of 7th grade. I can't even tell you how much stress and strain the teasing has placed on our family. We were really at a breaking point emotionally. The FOUR MINUTES A DAY project has literally changed his whole perception of school now and has changed our lives at home. He no longer walks in the door from school crying and hating school. He is actually happy." a mother

"Before this alliance was formed, I thought I would have lost hope. Kids were constantly teasing me ... and I was even considering missing school! Once you stepped in with this program, those problems were vanquished and done with. I feel safer now that I walk with students in the halls. Plus, I am even starting to make new friends. Thanks a ton for starting The FOUR MINUTES A DAY project." a 7th grader

"I realized the little things in life one may do, can make a big difference in someone else's life." a student volunteer

WITH GROUNDBREAKING INSIGHT INTO BULLYING, E.C. BERNARD OFFERS A PROVEN SOLUTION TO BULLIED STUDENTS FEELING ISOLATED AND AFRAID IN SCHOOL HALLWAYS.

ISBN 978-0-9793200-7-1

5 1 2 0 0

9 780979 320071

FOUR MINUTES A DAY

BY E.C. BERNARD

TYPO

THE INVOLVED PARENT'S
SEVENTH-GRADE GUIDE

BY
ELLEN SHRAGER

Integrity

Initiative,
Independence

The Myth of
Extracurricular
Activities

Self-Confidence

Disciplined
Work Habits

Respect Accorded
by Faculty

Reaction to Setbacks

Concern for Others

A Parental Wake-Up Call
to Make the Timely Transition from
Elementary School Manager
to Seventh-Grade Coach

Illustrated by Abby Bosley and Anthony T. Shelton, Sr.

"Edgy."

"Compelling – I couldn't stop reading it."

"Groundbreaking."

"Ellen Shrager is 'Super Nanny Jo'
to middle-school parents."

Many of today's involved parents are afraid of what will happen to their children if they don't have the right GPA or extracurricular activities when applying to college. Seventh grade parents need to broaden their focus and plan now for how their children will be rated on the "soft issues" on the Teacher Evaluation for the Common Application for colleges and universities: integrity, reaction to setbacks, and concern for others.

Use this book as a blueprint to avoid overshooting the role of "protective manager" of your elementary school children and to make the timely transition to the role of "coach" to your adolescent.

Take advantage of the grace period when grades and consequences do not impact college applications and teacher evaluations: seventh grade.

Seventh grade is the perfect time to let your child make mistakes. This willingness to let your child falter will go against your instinct to help create success, but will pay dividends in your child's future: scoring well on the Teacher Evaluation for college applications, staying in college, and keeping a job upon graduation.

Third Printing

Teacher Dialogues

by

Ellen Shrager

A Survival Guide to Successful Dialogues with

Low-Performing Students

Indulged Students

Enabling Parents

Cross-Generational Colleagues

Illustrated by Abby Bosley
and Anthony T. Shelton, Sr.

Dear Colleagues,

As I enter my 25th year of teaching, many changes in society continue to impact my classroom delivery in three ways:

💜STUDENTS - Five fundamental changes in society influence undesirable behaviors children bring to school. Learn how to build a bridge between where students are and where they need to be in order to function appropriately in the classroom. (See page 59.)

💜 PARENTS - Five different changes in society influence some parents to enable their children. Learn how to listen to enabling parents, discern their illusions, and compassionately offer facts to guide them to support appropriate consequences for their children's behavior and efforts. (See page 117.)

💜CROSS-GENERATIONAL COLLEAGUES - Similar changes contribute to miscommunication among the cross-generational teaching staff. There are ten implicit rules of conduct that should be made explicit, and can be the springboard for discussion for faculty meetings and for mentor meetings with new teachers. (See page 82)

What we teachers learned in our teacher preparatory courses represent the border of a large jigsaw puzzle — this book will help fill in the missing pieces.

Sincerely,
Ellen Shrager

ABOUT THE AUTHOR

**TO ORDER, OR FOR MORE INFORMATION
ON VOLUME DISCOUNTS, CALL
1 (610) 355-0553
E-MAIL: TEACHERVOICEPUBLISHING@comcast.net
P.O. BOX 446 VILLANOVA, PA 19085-0446**

TEACHER DIALOGUES	$20
THE INVOLVED PARENT'S 7TH GRADE GUIDE	$16
THE INVOLVED PARENT'S 9TH GRADE GUIDE	$16
THE INVOLVED PARENT'S 6TH GRADE GUIDE	$16
THE WORLD LANGUAGE DAILY TECH GUIDE	$20
FOUR MINUTES A DAY	$12

 Ellen Shrager is a full-time seventh-grade teacher in Pennsylvania. Previously she taught high school in New Hampshire and community college in Massachusetts.

Mrs. Shrager frequently keynotes state and regional conferences, leads workshops and sessions at national conventions such as ASCD, ASCA, NMSA, and ACTFL, and presents multiple school in-services.

She talks about the top 5 changes in society, how they impact the way students are raised, and the behaviors and skills students bring to the classroom. She inspires teachers to build a bridge between where the children are and where they need to be to function in the classroom. She helps teachers to discern parental illusions and engage in dialogues with parents in such a way that the parents support appropriate consequences for their children's behavior and effort.

Ellen. is currently exploring the best way for teachers to share their Daily Tech Guides.

Mrs. Shrager lives in Newtown Square, Pennsylvania, with her husband, Ed. For more information, go to: *www.ellenshrager.com.*